THE HIDDEN LIFE & BEAUTY *of* JESUS

A 28 DAY DEVOTIONAL

Rachel Wenke
Copyright © 2016

The Hidden Life & Beauty of Jesus: A 28 day devotional
Rachel Wenke
Copyright © 2016

No part of this publication may be reproduced or transmitted in any form or by any means, electronic or mechanical, including photocopy, recording, or any information storage or retrieval system, without permission in writing from the author. All scripture quotations, unless otherwise indicated, are taken from the New King James Version®. Copyright © 1982, Thomas Nelson, Inc. Used by permission. All rights reserved. Scripture quotations marked (AMP) are taken from the AMPLIFIED® BIBLE, Copyright © 1954, 1958, 1962, 1964, 1965, 1987 by the Lockman Foundation Used by Permission. (www.Lockman.org). Scripture quotations marked (NLT) are taken from the Holy Bible, New Living Translation, copyright © 1996, 2004, 2007 by Tyndale House Foundation. Used by permission of Tyndale House Publishers, Inc., Carol Stream, Illinois 60188. All rights reserved. Scripture quotations marked (TPT) are taken from the Psalms: Poetry on fire. The Passion Translation® or Song of Songs: Divine Romance, The Passion Translation®, Copyright © 2014, 2015, Used by permission of BroadStreet Publishing Group, LLC, Racine, Wisconsin, USA. www.thepassiontranslation.com. All rights reserved.

National Library of Australia Cataloguing-in-Publication entry
Creator: Wenke, Rachel, author
Title: The hidden life and beauty of Jesus: a 28 day devotional/ Rachel Wenke
ISBN: 9780994273437 (paperback)
Subjects: Glory of God-Christianity, Jesus Christ, Jesus Christ- Devotional literature
Dewey Number: 231.

Front cover floral artwork by Victoria Highet
www.victoriahighet.bigcartel.com
Instagram: victoria highet

Acknowledgements to Daniel Jurekie for his technical assistance in formatting the book cover.

Printed and bound in Australia.
facebook.com/hiddenlifeandbeautyofJesus

CONTENTS

Preface 5

Day 1: True Life 7

Day 2: Dine with Me 10

Day 3: Unveiling My Beauty 13

Day 4: Masterpiece 15

Day 5: In My Eyes 17

Day 6: My Hands 19

Day 7: Do I Compel You? 22

Day 8: Calling You By Name 25

Day 9: Colour 28

Day 10: Dimness Fades 31

Day 11: Green Pastures 34

Day 12: Scarlet Blood 37

Day 13: White as Snow 40

Day 14: Morning Star 42

Day 15: By My Spirit 45

Day 16: Mesmerise 48

Day 17: I Am the Door 50

Day 18: Seek to Enter Deeper 57

Day 19: My Increase Shall Never End 56

Day 20: My Name is Wonderful 58

Day 21: The Abundance of My Heart 61

Day 22: I Want to Romance You 64
Day 23: My Beautiful Song 67
Day 24: My Garden 69
Day 25: Inner Beauty 72
Day 26: The Greatest Separation 75
Day 27: To Know Me is to Fear Me 77
Day 28: I AM THE WAY 80
Your Invitation to Know Jesus Christ 83
Other Books by this Author 89

PREFACE
"Who is this King of glory?..."
Psalm 24:10

Who is Jesus? If all the books ever written in history were to describe the glory and beauty of Jesus, they would only capture a glimpse of the magnitude of who He is. The glorious Person of Jesus Christ is far more wonderful than the human language could ever begin to express. In the same way, the purpose of this devotional is not to attempt to give you a complete revelation of who Jesus is. Rather, each message of this book, written in the First Person of the Lord Jesus, was inspired by the Holy Spirit to simply awaken your own desire to seek out for yourself who this King of glory is.

Jesus, who loves you with an everlasting love, longs for you to know and experience who He is more deeply, so you may enjoy a stronger and more intimate relationship with Him. As you read each devotional message and meditate on the related Scriptures, may the Holy Spirit draw you more deeply into the glorious Presence of Jesus. May you embark on a daily journey of delight as you lay aside your life and discover the splendour and beauty of His (Matthew 16:25).

One thing I have asked of the LORD,
and that I will seek:
That I may dwell in the house of the LORD
[in His presence] all the days of my life,
To gaze upon the beauty
[the delightful loveliness and majestic grandeur]
of the LORD
And to meditate in His temple.

Psalm 27:4 (AMP)

DAY 1:

TRUE LIFE

"'for in Him we live and move and have our being..."
Acts 17:28

There is a vibrancy, vitality and beauty in Me that the world does not know and cannot manufacture. When you meet with Me, you meet with life itself. I am the Giver of all things, and in Me and through Me all things exist and have their being. How then do you think that you can live separate from Me?

You are not truly living until you are meeting with Me. You have not truly known beauty or delight until you have met with Me. Each day, you are not truly living unless you meet with Me and allow My life to flow through you by My Spirit. True life, true satisfaction, and the greatest contentment and delight comes from meeting with Me, knowing Me, and allowing My life to flow through you.

The strength and vitality and depth of life that is in Me is so great that it will transform you. When you meet with Me and My life, and see My glory and behold who I am, My holiness, My beauty and My Majesty, it is impossible not to be changed. The longer you behold Me, gazing upon who I am, the greater this transformation will be by My Spirit.

As you allow My life to exchange with yours and allow My life to flow through you, you will be continually refreshed and renewed. There is nothing that My life cannot overcome. This is how I want you to live every day. This is how you were made to live. You cannot live separate from Me and stay refreshed. You cannot live separate from Me and have true joy or contentment. Apart from Me, you can do nothing. All life comes from Me. I want you to live every day with the vibrancy of My life flowing through you like electricity, empowering you daily to do the Father's will.

Do you want to experience the glorious life I have waiting for you? Why do you hold onto your life when you can have Mine? Come and receive My life and vitality. Come and meet with My glory. COME AND MEET WITH ME.

SEE ALSO:

1 John 5:12
He who has the Son has life; he who does not have the Son of God does not have life.

2 Corinthians 3:17-18
Now the Lord is the Spirit; and where the Spirit of the Lord is, there is liberty. But we all, with unveiled face, beholding as in a mirror the glory of the Lord, are being transformed into the same image from glory to glory, just as by the Spirit of the Lord.

John 15:5
I am the vine, you are the branches. He who abides in Me, and I in him, bears much fruit; for without Me you can do nothing.

DAY 2:

DINE WITH ME

"Come, all you who are thirsty, come to the waters; and you who have no money, come, buy and eat! Come, buy wine and milk without money and without cost. Why spend money on what is not bread, and your labor on what does not satisfy? Listen, listen to me, and eat what is good, and you will delight in the richest of fare"
Isaiah 55:1-2

Dine with Me. I want to gaze at you across the table as we dine together at the banquet I have prepared for you. Do you know what I have in store for you as we dine together? Do you know the delights I have for you?

I want your soul to feast on the abundance of who I AM. I want your senses to feast on My fullness, as you surrender to My Spirit who will make your senses towards Me come alive. I want your eyes to feast on the beauty of the light and glory that is in My heart. I want your taste to be overcome with the sweetness of My Word, My rich Presence and My deep desire for you. I want your ears to be captivated by the sound of My gentle voice whispering in your ear. Let your heart feast on Me. Let your heart be overwhelmed by Me as you dine with Me and feast on the riches of My glory.

I want you to dine with Me, but you must first let Me into your heart and make room for Me, for I do not want to dine with an absent shell, but with who you are - your heart. I want all of your heart at the table with Me. Who wants to dine with a distracted party? Is this true fellowship? Dine with Me, but give Me all of your heart so you may truly delight in the feast I have prepared for you. Come and dine with Me now, My Father has a seat prepared just for you.

SEE ALSO:

Revelation 3:20
Behold, I stand at the door and knock. If anyone hears My voice and opens the door, I will come in to him and dine with him, and he with Me.

Psalm 36:8
They are abundantly satisfied with the fullness of Your house, And You give them drink from the river of Your pleasures.

Psalm 119:103
How sweet are Your words to my taste,
Sweeter than honey to my mouth!

Luke 14:15-18
Now when one of those who sat at the table with Him heard these things, he said to Him, "Blessed is he who shall eat bread in

the kingdom of God!" Then He said to him, "A certain man gave a great supper and invited many, and sent his servant at supper time to say to those who were invited, 'Come, for all things are now ready.' But they all with one accord began to make excuses...

Matthew 20:23
So He said to them, "You will indeed drink My cup, and be baptized with the baptism that I am baptized with; but to sit on My right hand and on My left is not Mine to give, but it is for those for whom it is prepared by My Father."

DAY 3:

UNVEILING MY BEAUTY

"One thing I have asked of the LORD, and that I will seek: That I may dwell in the house of the LORD [in His presence] all the days of my life, To gaze upon the beauty [the delightful loveliness and majestic grandeur] of the LORD And to meditate in His temple"
Psalm 27:4 (AMP)

Why do I hide My beauty from the world? Because she does not treasure it. She cannot see it. Only those that give something of themselves will see My beauty. It costs you to see My beauty and My glory. The more you give of yourself, the more you will see of Me. The more My life will be seen through you.

Why do you not see Me? Why do you not hear Me? Why do you not sense Me? It is not because I cannot be found. It is because you are seeking other things. You have put greater worth on other things. The more you wonder of Me, the more you will see Me as the greatest wonder this universe has or ever will know. Then you will not be able to take your eyes off of Me, just as I can't take My eyes off you. Fix your eyes on Me. It is easy to fix your eyes on Me when you are beholding My life and beauty. As you treasure what you see in Me above all else, more will be revealed.

SEE ALSO:

Matthew 13:44
Again, the kingdom of heaven is like treasure hidden in a field, which a man found and hid; and for joy over it he goes and sells all that he has and buys that field.

Luke 9: 23-24
Then He said to them all, "If anyone desires to come after Me, let him deny himself, and take up his cross daily, and follow Me. For whoever desires to save his life will lose it, but whoever loses his life for My sake will save it.

Jeremiah 29:13
And you will seek Me and find Me, when you search for Me with all your heart.

Hebrews 12:2 (AMP)
[looking away from all that will distract us and] focusing our eyes on Jesus, who is the Author and Perfecter of faith...

DAY 4:

MASTERPIECE

> *"For it is the God who commanded light to shine out of darkness, who has shone in our hearts to give the light of the knowledge of the glory of God in the face of Jesus Christ. But we have this treasure in earthen vessels, that the excellence of the power may be of God and not of us."*
> 2 Corinthians 4:6-7

I have already painted My very nature, a spectacular Masterpiece that is beyond comparison to anything in heaven or earth onto the very fabric of your heart. Such rich depths of colour, bold design, and intricate, exquisite detail have been imprinted onto your very heart, before the foundation of the world.

As you surrender to Me, this Masterpiece is slowly and surely being unveiled, and you and those around you will begin to see what I have painted in you. The unveiling of this Masterpiece in your heart is simply the unveiling of My glory that already lives in you by My Spirit. Like a sackcloth hiding all the splendour of heaven so is your soulish, fleshly nature hiding the beautiful Masterpiece that I have painted on your heart by My Spirit. This Masterpiece is Me. Do you want to see what I have painted already on your heart? Do you want to see Me? My glory is already painted within your heart. Let Me take away the sackcloth so that it may be revealed.

SEE ALSO:

Ephesians 2:10 (AMP)
For we are His workmanship [His own master work, a work of art], created in Christ Jesus [reborn from above—spiritually transformed, renewed, ready to be used] for good works, which God prepared [for us]...

Ephesians 1:3-4
Blessed be the God and Father of our Lord Jesus Christ, who has blessed us with every spiritual blessing in the heavenly places in Christ, just as He chose us in Him before the foundation of the world, that we should be holy and without blame before Him in love,

2 Corinthians 3:18
But we all, with unveiled face, beholding as in a mirror the glory of the Lord, are being transformed into the same image from glory to glory, just as by the Spirit of the Lord.

Psalm 30:11
You have turned for me my mourning into dancing; You have put off my sackcloth and clothed me with gladness,

DAY 5:

IN MY EYES

"His eyes were like a flame of fire…"
Revelation 19:12

Look into My eyes and see the depth of My longing for you. Look into My eyes and see how I am yearning, even now for you. For My eyes are burning completely with love and passion and desire for you. They are aflame for you.

My eyes are wide open right now, and they are looking at you. Do you want to look into My eyes? For I am looking into yours. When you look into My eyes, you will see My heart. You will see the life that is within Me. You will see pools of Living Water. You will see life; you will see forgiveness. You will see mercy. You will see peace. Most of all, you will see love. And you will find that deep within My love, you are surrounded by Me. For you are the apple of My eye. The central focus of My heart.

Do not simply glance into My eyes, gaze upon them. Allow them to draw you into My heart. Journey deeply into My heart as you gaze into My eyes. Immerse yourself in the pools of Living Water inside of Me. Refresh and revitalise your soul in the life and newness found within Me by the Holy Spirit. Saturate yourself with My love and devotion for you.

SEE ALSO:

Deuteronomy 32:10
He found him in a desert land
And in the wasteland, a howling wilderness;
He encircled him, He instructed him,
He kept him as the apple of His eye.

Psalm 34:15
The eyes of the LORD are on the righteous,
And His ears are open to their cry.

Song of Solomon 8:6
Set me as a seal upon your heart,
As a seal upon your arm;
For love is as strong as death,
Jealousy as cruel as the grave;
Its flames are flames of fire,
A most vehement flame.

John 4:13-14
Jesus answered and said to her, "Whoever drinks of this water will thirst again, but whoever drinks of the water that I shall give him will never thirst. But the water that I shall give him will become in him a fountain of water springing up into everlasting life."

DAY 6:

MY HANDS

"For I, the L<small>ORD</small> your God, will hold your right hand, Saying to you, 'Fear not, I will help you.'"
Isaiah 41:13

My hands have been and were always in existence before the beginning of time. My hands helped fashion the earth, the stars, the sun and the moon. With My fingertips, I moulded the mountains and valleys that you see today. With the palms of My hands, I smoothed over the sands and oceans and the surfaces of billions upon billions of planets in the universe.

With these same hands, My Father fashioned you and moulded you while you were in your mother's womb. He made you in the perfect image of Myself. Together with the Holy Spirit, We created you with Our very hands.

These same hands of Mine were the hands that were punctured, beaten, pierced and nailed to a cross. My same hands were brutally battered, bruised and bled for you. But when I felt those nails drive into My flesh, the pain was overshadowed by a longing and desire in Me that one day these same hands of Mine would be able to hold yours. These same hands would one day be able to carry you.

How I long to hold your hands. How I long for My hands to carry you. Will you take My hand that is reaching out to you now?

SEE ALSO:

Psalm 119:73
Your hands have made me and fashioned me…

Hebrews 1:10
And: "You, LORD, in the beginning laid the foundation of the earth, And the heavens are the work of Your hands.

John 1:1-3
In the beginning was the Word, and the Word was with God, and the Word was God. He was in the beginning with God. All things were made through Him, and without Him nothing was made that was made.

John 20:25 (AMP)
So the other disciples kept telling him, "We have seen the Lord!" But he said to them, "Unless I see in His hands the marks of the nails, and put my finger into the nail prints, and put my hand into His side, I will never believe [it].."

Isaiah 53:5
But He was wounded for our transgressions,

He was bruised for our iniquities;
The chastisement for our peace was upon Him,
And by His stripes we are healed.

Isaiah 41:10
Fear not, for I am with you;
Be not dismayed, for I am your God.
I will strengthen you,
Yes, I will help you,
I will uphold you with My righteous right hand.'

DAY 7:

DO I COMPEL YOU?

"looking unto Jesus, the author and finisher of our faith, who for the joy that was set before Him endured the cross, despising the shame, and has sat down at the right hand of the throne of God."
Hebrews 12:2

I was compelled by such love for you that I beared the agony of dying on the cross. But I didn't endure it begrudgingly; I did it with joy, for I saw the end from the beginning! I saw the start of our life together with no separation coming between us. Do you know what My eyes were fixed on as I was on that cross? You and only you.

The Roman soldiers did not hold back when they tortured Me. My suffering was greater than what any man should ever endure. I was physically marred beyond recognition of any human form. I was mocked and despised and spat on. My very beard was plucked from My face. Yet through all this, as I was dying on the cross, as My body was writhing in pain, do you know what I was thinking of? It was not, "Make it stop; make the pain go away". I was thinking, "Soon we will be together; soon we will be as one. Soon, nothing will separate you and I." That is what compelled Me to the cross, My love for the Father and My love for you.

So many today are compelled by the world, by its gratifications, its fleeting pleasures. My compelling passion for you overrides all other passions this world may offer you. How I long for you to be compelled by Me. Do My life and love compel you? Or are you compelled by other things? Come and begin to understand My love for you and the price I paid for you, and be compelled.

SEE ALSO:

Isaiah 52:14 (NLT)
But many were amazed when they saw him. His face was so disfigured he seemed hardly human, and from his appearance, one would scarcely know he was a man.

John 3:16 (AMP)
For God so [greatly] loved and dearly prized the world, that He [even] gave His [One and] only begotten Son, so that whoever believes and trusts in Him [as Savior] shall not perish, but have eternal life.

1 John 4:10 (NLT)
This is real love—not that we loved God, but that he loved us and sent his Son as a sacrifice to take away our sins.

Romans 8:38-39 (AMP)

For I am convinced [and continue to be convinced—beyond any doubt] that neither death, nor life, nor angels, nor principalities, nor things present and threatening, nor things to come, nor powers, nor height, nor depth, nor any other created thing, will be able to separate us from the [unlimited] love of God, which is in Christ Jesus our Lord.

DAY 8:

CALLING YOU BY NAME

*"But now, thus says the LORD, who created you, O Jacob,
And He who formed you, O Israel:
Fear not, for I have redeemed you;
I have called you by your name; You are Mine.'"*

Isaiah 43:1

My Beloved, do you know that I am always calling out to you. I am saying, "Come. Come to Me." I am forever calling your name unto Me. I am longing for you to hear My call unto you. Can you hear it now? I am calling your name. I am longing for you respond to My calling unto you, for you to turn your affection to Me; to come unto Me.

You will hear Me beckoning unto you when you seek My face. You cannot hear Me calling your name when your attention is not on Me, for My voice is only known in My Presence. The moment you bring your attention and focus to Me, then you may know My voice. My voice is not usually audible or heard with your ears, though I may choose to reveal it this way by My Spirit. My voice is most often a gentle whisper that is only known by your heart. It is the most beautiful sound your heart can ever listen to- My voice beckoning you unto Me. My voice is always calling your name. It is always calling you closer to Me. My voice on this earth is My Spirit and what a beautiful voice He is.

Do you know My voice? Can you perceive it? I am speaking right now to your heart. Quieten yourself, so you can hear Me and listen to My words. Surrender to Me and come closer to My heart to hear what I am speaking to you right this moment. Come closer and know My voice more intimately. My voice unto you is the most glorious sound your heart can ever hear. I am calling you by name now. Can you hear Me?

SEE ALSO:

John 10:3-4
To him the doorkeeper opens, and the sheep hear his voice; and he calls his own sheep by name and leads them out. And when he brings out his own sheep, he goes before them; and the sheep follow him, for they know his voice

Hebrews 3:14-15
For we have become partakers of Christ if we hold the beginning of our confidence steadfast to the end, while it is said: "Today, if you will hear His voice, Do not harden your hearts as in the rebellion."

Revelation 22:17

And the Spirit and the bride say, "Come!" And let him who hears say, "Come!" And let him who thirsts come. Whoever desires, let him take the water of life freely.

DAY 9:

COLOUR

"Then God said, 'let there be light', and there was light. And God saw the light and it was good; and God divided the light from the darkness."
Genesis 1:3-4

Why do you think My Father made light? Was it so that He could see the world? We could already see everything without light and colour, for We do not see with natural vision. We created light for you so that you could see contrasts. For this same reason, We created colour. We made colour for you so that you could see distinction and contrast in Our creation.

Colour and light are what you perceive with your senses, but the colour and light that surrounds Me are much more than you can see with your eyes. True colour and light are sensed also in your inner being bearing witness with what is in you. I have placed the brightest, purest rainbow of My glory deep inside you now.

As you look into My light that is in you now, so the distinction and contrasts begin to be evident. So the world and its seeming colours are seen for what they are. The brightness of the world begins to fade and only the brightness and manifold colour and vibrant richness of who I am remains. The light of who I am will never grow dim or fade. This light that is in Me, this light who is Me, is brighter than the sun, more intense than any morning light.

The brightness that is within Me is not of this world. I am not of this world and cannot be compared to any other. Look within and begin to soak in My radiance. I am in you, the eternal and true hope of glory.

SEE ALSO:

Ezekiel 1:27-28
Also from the appearance of His waist and upward I saw, as it were, the color of amber with the appearance of fire all around within it; and from the appearance of His waist and downward I saw, as it were, the appearance of fire with brightness all around. Like the appearance of a rainbow in a cloud on a rainy day, so was the appearance of the brightness all around it. This was the appearance of the likeness of the glory of the LORD...

Revelation 21:23
The city had no need of the sun or of the moon to shine in it, for the glory of God illuminated it. The Lamb is its light.

Revelation 4:2-3

Immediately I was in the Spirit; and behold, a throne set in heaven, and One sat on the throne. And He who sat there was like a jasper and a sardius stone in appearance; and there was a rainbow around the throne, in appearance like an emerald.

Colossians 1:27

To them God willed to make known what are the riches of the glory of this mystery among the Gentiles: which is Christ in you, the hope of glory.

DAY 10:

DIMNESS FADES

"The sun shall no longer be your light by day,
Nor for brightness shall the moon give light to you;
But the LORD will be to you an everlasting light,
And your God your glory. Your sun shall no longer go down,
Nor shall your moon withdraw itself;
For the LORD will be your everlasting light,
And the days of your mourning shall be ended.
Also your people shall all be righteous;
They shall inherit the land forever,
The branch of My planting, The work of My hands,
That I may be glorified."
Isaiah 60:19-21

How dimly the world sees right now. How dimly they are peering. Yet even My friends and My family here on earth see so dimly. They are peering through dark clouded glass. Do you know where brightness comes from? Do you know where the dimness ceases and brightness enters? It is when you behold My glory. You see dimly because you see through your natural senses, your limited soulish realm- the realm of this fallen age. But when you seek My face and begin to see as I see, so this dimness fades and the light and power of My glory illuminate your path.

Behold My glory and watch the brightness of My rising come upon you. Watch the brightness of who I am

begin to saturate and colour your world around you. For now all you will see is glory! Now you will see that truly the earth is full of My glory, for you are seeing through Me and My glory. Yet still, on this earth, you will only every taste glimpses of the fullness and wonder that are waiting for you in heaven. No eye has seen or ear heard what is in store for you in glory. But you can see a glimpse now. Do you want to see a glimpse of the brightness of My glory? Seek Me now.

SEE ALSO:

Isaiah 60; 1-3,5
Arise, shine; For your light has come!
And the glory of the LORD is risen upon you.
For behold, the darkness shall cover the earth,
And deep darkness the people;
But the LORD will arise over you,
And His glory will be seen upon you.
The Gentiles shall come to your light,
And kings to the brightness of your rising.
Then you shall see and become radiant,
And your heart shall swell with joy...

Isaiah 6:3
And one cried to another and said:
"Holy, holy, holy is the LORD of hosts;
The whole earth is full of His glory!"

1 Corinthians 13:12
For now we see in a mirror, dimly, but then face to face. Now I know in part, but then I shall know just as I also am known.

2 Corinthians 3:18 (AMP)
And we all, with unveiled face, continually seeing as in a mirror the glory of the Lord, are progressively being transformed into His image from [one degree of] glory to [even more] glory, which comes from the Lord, [who is] the Spirit.

1 Corinthians 2:9 (NLT)
That is what the Scriptures mean when they say,
"No eye has seen, no ear has heard, and no mind has imagined what God has prepared for those who love him."

John 8:12
Then Jesus spoke to them again, saying, "I am the light of the world. He who follows Me shall not walk in darkness, but have the light of life."

DAY 11:

GREEN PASTURES

"He makes me to lie down in green pastures…"
Psalm 23:2

Green is the colour of life. The world is always looking for greener pastures, for they want more from their life but they are always searching. They do not realise that the greenest pastures are only and will only ever be found in Me. I bring you to the greenest pastures of your life where you will find true rest for your soul. Where you can release the tensions and stirrings of your mind and just breathe in My goodness. Do you want to enjoy the greenest, freshest, softest, most luscious pastures where you can lie and rest in total peace knowing I have taken care of all? I want you to lie down and rest with Me in the green pastures within My heart, in My Presence.

Let My light shine down upon your face as you look to Me, basking in the radiance of My Presence beaming down on you and radiating through you. Stop searching for greener pastures elsewhere. Whatever you are looking for is in Me now. Come and kick off your shoes, kick off your fears, your worries and your burdens and come and lie here with Me. There is a green pasture already prepared for you to come and enjoy. Come now, and I will give you rest.

SEE ALSO:

Matt 11:28-30 (NLT)
Then Jesus said, "Come to me, all of you who are weary and carry heavy burdens, and I will give you rest. Take my yoke upon you. Let me teach you, because I am humble and gentle at heart, and you will find rest for your souls. For my yoke is easy to bear, and the burden I give you is light."

Psalm 4:6-8 (TPT)
... Let the light of Your radiant face Break through and shine down upon us! The joy You give me is far greater than the gladness of harvest time...Now I can lay down in peace and fall asleep, For no matter what happens, my confidence is found in You!

Hebrews 4:9-10 (AMP)
So there remains a [full and complete] Sabbath rest for the people of God. For the one who has once entered His rest has also rested from [the weariness and pain of] his [human] labors, just as God rested from [those labors uniquely] His own.

Song of Solomon 1:16 (TPT)
My Beloved One,
You are pleasing beyond words,
And so winsome!
Our resting place is anointed and flourishing,
Like a green forest meadow bathed in light.

Numbers 6:25-26 (AMP)
The LORD make His face shine upon you [with favor],
And be gracious to you [surrounding you with lovingkindness];
The LORD lift up His countenance (face) upon you [with divine approval], And give you peace [a tranquil heart and life].

DAY 12:

SCARLET BLOOD

"But now in Christ Jesus you who once were far off have been brought near by the blood of Christ."
Ephesians 2:13

The most beautiful colour My Father and I ever created, is the colour of My blood. For My blood being poured out for you was the Father's love flowing out of My being unto yours. My blood represents My love for you. You are so precious, so dear to Me that I gave My body, My own flesh and blood for you while you did not know Me. My blood has brought you near to Me.

My blood is My liquid love. When you sin and fall away from Me, I beckon you to turn to Me so I can cover your sins with My blood. For when I cover you with My blood, I am covering you with My love. When you are turning to My blood, you are turning to My love and the Father's love, by My Precious Spirit.

As I hung on the cross and My blood was seeping from My body, I had you on My heart. I could see who I was gaining in what I was losing- I was gaining you! My blood brought you into My Kingdom, and only My blood keeps you there. Without it, you cannot be near to Me. Without it, there is a veil of sin between you and the Father. By My blood and the power of the Spirit, you are made white as snow- righteous, holy and blameless. Nothing is between us. Can you see now why the most beautiful colour is the colour of My blood? For it brings you closer to Me.

SEE ALSO:

Romans 5:9-11 (NLT)
And since we have been made right in God's sight by the blood of Christ, he will certainly save us from God's condemnation. For since our friendship with God was restored by the death of his Son while we were still his enemies, we will certainly be saved through the life of his Son. So now we can rejoice in our wonderful new relationship with God because our Lord Jesus Christ has made us friends of God.

Colossians 1: 19-20
For it pleased the Father that in Him all the fullness should dwell, and by Him to reconcile all things to Himself, by Him, whether things on earth or things in heaven, having made peace through the blood of His cross.

Hebrews 10:19-22 (NLT)
And so, dear brothers and sisters, we can boldly enter heaven's Most Holy Place because of the blood of Jesus. By his death, Jesus opened a new and life-giving way through the curtain into the Most Holy Place. And since we have a great High Priest who rules

over God's house, let us go right into the presence of God with sincere hearts fully trusting him. For our guilty consciences have been sprinkled with Christ's blood to make us clean, and our bodies have been washed with pure water.

DAY 13:

WHITE AS SNOW

*"'Come now, and let us reason together,"
Says the LORD,
'Though your sins are like scarlet,
They shall be as white as snow;
Though they are red like crimson,
They shall be as wool.'"*
Isaiah 1:18

When I wash you with My blood, I wash you inside and out. I make you white as snow, entirely clean. It doesn't matter what you've done. It doesn't matter how deep the wounds, how dark the stain of sin is on your life; how dark the spot. It is all cleaned white as snow when My blood washes you. You become the righteousness of God, like Me. In Me is no spot, in Me is no blemish, no darkness. There will be no trace of stain left on you, only righteousness, for you and I become one, and only righteousness is found in Me.

Come and be washed by My blood. Let Me purify you and cleanse you with My righteousness. I want to wash you, the deepest parts of your heart with My blood. Let Me wash you every day in My blood. Then you will see and live through My righteous garments which I clothe you with. You will see that My blood has made you white as snow. I see no spot on you.

SEE ALSO:

2 Corinthians 5:21
For He made Him who knew no sin to be sin for us, that we might become the righteousness of God in Him.

Song of Solomon 4:7
You are all fair, my love, And there is no spot in you

Hebrews 9:13-14
For if the blood of bulls and goats and the ashes of a heifer, sprinkling the unclean, sanctifies for the purifying of the flesh, how much more shall the blood of Christ, who through the eternal Spirit offered Himself without spot to God, cleanse your conscience from dead works to serve the living God?

1 John 1:7 (AMP)
but if we [really] walk in the Light [that is, live each and every day in conformity with the precepts of God], as He Himself is in the Light, we have [true, unbroken] fellowship with one another [He with us, and we with Him], and the blood of Jesus His Son cleanses us from all sin [by erasing the stain of sin, keeping us cleansed from sin in all its forms and manifestations].

Ephesians 5: 26-27
that He might sanctify and cleanse her with the washing of water by the word, that He might present her to Himself a glorious church, not having spot or wrinkle or any such thing, but that she should be holy and without blemish.

DAY 14:

MORNING STAR

"I, Jesus, have sent My angel to testify to you these things in the churches. I am the Root and the Offspring of David, the Bright and Morning Star."
Revelation 22:16

There is something so precious, so beautiful about the morning that most on this earth will never truly realise. Each morning is a gift I have given. A gift to be prized and treasured. The beginning of a brand new day that I have authored for you. The beginning of life for another day. You see it in My creation each morning: fresh dew on the leaves, the sound of birds singing in the air, the sun rising with new brilliant colours illuminating the sky. All gifts are from Me but the greatest gift I bring every morning is the gift to come and know Me by My Spirit.

Seek Me in the morning when you are about to start your day. Just like every morning is new, so too are My mercies new every morning. My grace is new. My word for you is new. Every day I want to share the newness of My life with you. I want you to meet with Me. My grace is always new and waiting for you.

Don't wake up wishing you could fall back to sleep as the world. I created you to enjoy My gift of the morning. Rise early and enjoy the beautiful gift of the morning and the beautiful gift of knowing Me! Seek Me in the mornings and experience My newness! Seek Me, the Bright and Morning Star!

SEE ALSO:

Psalm 63:1
O God, You are my God; Early will I seek You...

Proverbs 8:17 (AMP)
I love those who love me;
And those who seek me early and diligently will find me

Psalm 5:3 (AMP)
In the morning, O LORD, You will hear my voice; In the morning I will prepare [a prayer and a sacrifice] for You and watch and wait [for You to speak to my heart].

Lamentations 3:22-23
Through the LORD's mercies we are not consumed, Because His compassions fail not. They are new every morning; Great is Your faithfulness.

Isaiah 43:18-19
Do not remember the former things,
Nor consider the things of old.
Behold, I will do a new thing,
Now it shall spring forth;
Shall you not know it?
I will even make a road in the wilderness
And rivers in the desert.

Luke 11:13
If you then, being evil, know how to give good gifts to your children, how much more will your heavenly Father give the Holy Spirit to those who ask Him!

DAY 15:

BY MY SPIRIT

*"The Spirit of the LORD is upon Me,
Because He has anointed Me
To preach the gospel to the poor;
He has sent Me to heal the brokenhearted,
To proclaim liberty to the captives
And recovery of sight to the blind,
To set at liberty those who are oppressed;
To proclaim the acceptable year of the LORD."*
Luke 4:18-19

If you want to meet with Me and experience who I am by My Presence and My Word, there is a Person you must come to know and depend on. This Person is the Holy Spirit. When I walked the earth, I lived every moment by the power of the Holy Spirit flowing through Me. It was by His power that multitudes were healed and delivered. It was by His power that I walked on water and performed mighty signs and wonders. It was by His power that I conquered all evil and was raised to life. Because I came to earth as a man, stripped of My divinity, I could never have performed what I did and fulfilled the Father's will without Him.

And so I say to you, without the Holy Spirit, you can never do the Father's will here on earth. Without Him, you cannot know Me, or commune with the Father or Me. The Holy Spirit was My Helper, My Comforter and My Friend when I walked the earth as a man, and today He is now on earth longing to be your Helper, your Comforter and your best Friend.

He will guide you into all things and the knowledge of who I am. The life and beauty of who I am can only be revealed through Him. Come to know the Holy Spirit and the life that is within Me will be gloriously revealed to you. He is waiting for you now to show you more of who I am.

SEE ALSO:

John 16:7, 13-15
Nevertheless I tell you the truth. It is to your advantage that I go away; for if I do not go away, the Helper will not come to you; but if I depart, I will send Him to you. However, when He, the Spirit of truth, has come, He will guide you into all truth; for He will not speak on His own authority, but whatever He hears He will speak; and He will tell you things to come. He will glorify Me, for He will take of what is Mine and declare it to you. All things that the Father has are Mine. Therefore I said that He will take of Mine and declare it to you.

Luke 4:14
Then Jesus returned in the power of the Spirit to Galilee, and news of Him went out through all the surrounding region.

Philippians 2:5-8
Let this mind be in you which was also in Christ Jesus, who, being in the form of God, did not consider it robbery to be equal with God, but made Himself of no reputation, taking the form of bondservant, and coming in the likeness of men. And being found in appearance as a man, He humbled Himself and became obedient to the point of death, even the death of the cross.

Zechariah 4:6
… 'Not by might nor by power, but by My Spirit,' Says the LORD of hosts.

DAY 16:

MESMERISE

*"Oh, worship the LORD in the beauty of holiness!
Tremble before Him, all the earth."*
Psalm 96:9

As you allow yourself to turn away from the impure noise and glitter of this world and turn to Me by the Spirit, something glorious will happen. Slowly but surely you will begin to see something that the world does not possess and does not know. You will sense the light, the contrast in Me that cannot be found in this world. It may start with you seeing merely a flicker, but you will sense it. Hunger for this contrast, for this very contrast that you are beginning to sense is the beauty of My Holiness.

The glimpse that you perceive may not seem like very much, but I only reveal to you what you treasure. The more you treasure this revelation of My being, the more My glory will intensify. The more attention you give to Me, the greater revelation of My glory you will receive. Fix your eyes on what you see of Me, no matter how small and it will grow. It will intensify and soon you will become more and more mesmerised by Me to the point where all else compared to Me will appear void of life and vitality. The key is to treasure what you see regardless how small and then what you see will grow. It is progressive, but it doesn't have to take you an eternity to grow in the revelation of Me. You can begin today.

Come now and turn away from the distractions of your life and meditate on Me. Let My Spirit reveal to you the purity, holiness and splendour of who I am, which cannot be compared with this world. Let Me begin to captivate and mesmerise you.

SEE ALSO:

Psalm 145:5
I will meditate on the glorious splendor of Your majesty, And on Your wondrous work

Psalm 50:2 (AMP)
Out of Zion, the perfection of beauty, God has shone forth.

Hebrews 12:1-2 (AMP)
Therefore, since we are surrounded by so great a cloud of witnesses [who by faith have testified to the truth of God's absolute faithfulness], stripping off every unnecessary weight and the sin which so easily and cleverly entangles us, let us run with endurance and active persistence the race that is set before us, looking away from all that will distract us and] focusing our eyes on Jesus, who is the Author and Perfecter of faith...

DAY 17:

I AM THE DOOR

*"Then Jesus said to them again,
'Most assuredly, I say to you, I am the door of the sheep.
All who ever came before Me are thieves and robbers,
but the sheep did not hear them. I am the door.
If anyone enters by Me, he will be saved, and will go in and
out and find pasture."
John 10:7-9*

I am the only door to eternal life. You cannot know My Father or enter the Kingdom of heaven without Me. The door of heaven is not locked. The door of heaven is open to all but to find this door you must find Me for I am the Door to heaven. I am the Door to eternity and there is no other way but through Me. My death and resurrection made an entrance into the Father's heart forevermore.

People try to pry their way into heaven on their own steam, through their own works, but they do not see that the door to heaven is a Person, it is I, Jesus Christ. They need to meet with Me. When will you know eternal life? When you know Me and enter Me in reality. When I am real to you, when I am more than just a doctrine or a prophet you read about or a wise sounding man. When you have met with Me, Jesus, the Living God, the Alpha and the Omega, Faithful and True, and continue to live in Me as your Lord, then you will know eternal life. My Spirit will show you the way to where I am. He will guide and lead you unto Me. But you must continually choose to walk My way through the open doors I give which lead to righteousness, and not through the doors of sin that the enemy places on your path to ensnare you.

Once you enter through the Door which is Me unto life everlasting, there is so much more that awaits you inside of Me. Within Me is the door to eternal life, but as you enter that door many more doors will be before you. Doors of opportunity, doors to greater revelations of My love, My peace, My joy, My rest, and My abundance. Doors to My wisdom, to My mercy, to My compassion, to My strength. Yet every one of these doors has even many more doors you can enter.

So enter through I, the Door to life, and then continue for the rest of your life entering deeper and deeper within the many doors and passages of My heart; the many doors of who I am. Each and every door is always unlocked; the doorways are open. You do not have to force your way in; they are waiting to be entered as you surrender to My Spirit.

SEE ALSO:

John 17:3
And this is eternal life, that they may know You, the only true God, and Jesus Christ whom You have sent.

John 14:6
Jesus said to him, "I am the way, the truth, and the life. No one comes to the Father except through Me.

John 10:1-3
"Most assuredly, I say to you, he who does not enter the sheepfold by the door, but climbs up some other way, the same is a thief and a robber. But he who enters by the door is the shepherd of the sheep. To him the doorkeeper opens, and the sheep hear his voice; and he calls his own sheep by name and leads them out.

DAY 18:
SEEK TO ENTER DEEPER

"Ask, and it will be given to you; seek, and you will find;
knock, and it will be opened to you.
For everyone who asks receives, and he who seeks finds,
and to him who knocks it will be opened."
Matthew 7:7-8

To enter the doors that are within Me more deeply, your heart must continually seek after Me. A heart that stops seeking after Me, ceases to enter deeper into My Presence. Doors may even appear shut to you, but it is only because you are not seeking Me with your whole heart. Your heart is divided and seeking many other things. When your heart is seeking after Me with a pure undivided heart, open doors that you did not know existed will begin to appear before you. Doors to deeper levels of My Presence, doors to greater levels of My peace and joy.

So come in through the door which I have opened for you now, but do not stop there. Always seek to journey deeper within the beautiful highways of love, grace and mercy within Me, and you will find a manifold array of doors waiting to be entered. When you enter a door within My heart, then you may lead others to this part of My nature by My Spirit.

Come, journey deep within Me. Deep inside the corridors of My Majesty and splendour. The corridors within My heart are not cramped or sterile like the corridors of the world; they are vast, beautiful, expansive fields progressively more glorious the deeper you journey in. Come journey within Me. Come enter through the doors of My heart waiting to be discovered!

SEE ALSO:

Matthew 5:8
Blessed are the pure in heart, For they shall see God.

Psalm 119:1-3
Blessed are the undefiled in the way,
Who walk in the law of the Lord!
Blessed are those who keep His testimonies,
Who seek Him with the whole heart!
They also do no iniquity;
They walk in His ways.

Psalm 18:19 (AMP)
He brought me out into a broad place; He rescued me because He was pleased with me and delighted in me.

Psalm 78:23
Yet He had commanded the clouds above,
And opened the doors of heaven,

DAY 19:

MY INCREASE SHALL NEVER END

*"Of the increase of His government and peace
There will be no end..."*
Isaiah 9:7

When you come to know Me, you will come to realise that your revelation of Me can forever be increasing. It never has to end. You cannot ever reach the pinnacle of knowledge and revelation of who I am. For as long as you have breath, you will never truly grasp the magnitude of My glory, My Majesty, My beauty, My peace and My power. The revelation of who I am will forever increase, and its increase will have no end.

When I walked the earth, I performed mighty feats and miracles as the Spirit came upon Me. But do you know you can do even greater? For you can grow in greater revelation, anointing and power by My Spirit. The glory on your life will always increase as your revelation of My glory increases in your life. Am I increasing in your life? Is the revelation of who I am growing? As your revelation of Me increases, so will My glory increase upon you.

SEE ALSO:

2 Corinthians 3:18 (AMP)
And we all, with unveiled face, continually seeing as in a mirror the glory of the Lord, are progressively being transformed into His image from [one degree of] glory to [even more] glory, which comes from the Lord, [who is] the Spirit.

John 14:12
"Most assuredly, I say to you, he who believes in Me, the works that I do he will do also; and greater works than these he will do, because I go to My Father.

Romans 11:33
Oh, the depth of the riches both of the wisdom and knowledge of God! How unsearchable are His judgments and His ways past finding out!

Isaiah 40:28
Have you not known? Have you not heard?
The everlasting God, the Lord,
The Creator of the ends of the earth,
Neither faints nor is weary.
His understanding is unsearchable.

DAY 20:

MY NAME IS WONDERFUL

*"For unto us a Child is born,
Unto us a Son is given;
And the government will be upon His shoulder.
And His name will be called
Wonderful, Counselor, Mighty God,
Everlasting Father, Prince of Peace."*
Isaiah 9:6

Wonderful is not merely a word used to describe Me; it is who I am, for I *AM* Wonderful. Every part of Me, every layer of My nature, every facet of who I AM is full of wonders this world cannot measure. The wonders found within Me are without comprehension. All of Me is wonderful. All of Me is wondrous.

In the world, you may experience pleasures, but you must realise that all the satisfactions that the world has to offer, no matter how gratifying, are only fleeting. They are momentary. The delight and wonder found in Me never ends. It is eternal. In Me are rivers of delight, continual streams of pleasure that you can be immersed in. The delights and wonder you come to experience will never cease! What awe awaits in Me! What wonders to behold!

But do you know what I do with Myself and My wonder? What I do with all that I am? I do not just display My wonder in the heavens. I came to earth and died and rose again so that I can share My wonder with you; so that I could make you Wonderful like Me; so that you could be full of wonder, by being filled with My Spirit. Now all of you is wonderful, for whatever My blood touches is made perfect, complete, and wonderful. You, My bride, are wonderful! Now when you abide in Me, you, My bride, are full of wonders incomprehensible; wonders that man cannot measure!

Everything I create, everything that comes from Me is truly wonderful. You cannot find a part of Me that will not inspire wonder in you. Each part of Me you discover will only ever get more and more wonderful. The more you begin to know Me, the more wonder you will see in Me. The more you see My wonder, the more you will see that the same wonder in Me is actually living in you by My Spirit! Come, enter into the wonder of who I AM and let My wonders flow through you.

SEE ALSO:

Judges 13: 17-18
Then Manoah said to the Angel of the LORD, "What is Your name, that when Your words come to pass we may honor You?" And the Angel of the LORD said to him, "Why do you ask My name, seeing it is wonderful?"

Psalm 139:6, 14
Such knowledge is too wonderful for me;
It is high, I cannot attain it...
I will praise You, for I am fearfully and wonderfully made
Marvelous are Your works,
And that my soul knows very well.

Daniel 4:2-3
I thought it good to declare the signs and wonders that the Most High God has worked for me.
How great are His signs,
And how mighty His wonders!
His kingdom is an everlasting kingdom,
And His dominion is from generation to generation.

Acts 5:12
And through the hands of the apostles
many signs and wonders were done among the people...

DAY 21:

THE ABUNDANCE OF MY HEART

"The thief does not come except to steal, and to kill, and to destroy. I have come that they may have life, and that they may have it more abundantly."
John 10:10

You will never truly know the fullness of My abundance until you experience My glory in the abundance of heaven. Even in heaven, the abundance you sense will continue to increase as you receive deeper revelations of the unspeakable glory which I radiate. You will experience such richness of sights, feelings and sounds, with senses that you have not known here on earth. But you do not need to wait until heaven; you can begin to taste the abundance of heaven here on earth, for such glorious abundance is found in Me by My Spirit. It is found within My heart.

Do you know that I can overwhelm earth's entire population into a state of total shock and awe if they were to see just a momentary flash of the glory and power that is laid up within Me? But while I love to startle the multitudes with the Spirit's power, My ultimate desire is that they come to Me so I may display to them personally the abundance of who I am- the abundance of My heart to theirs.

As you learn to follow Me, you will also experience My abundance overflow outwardly in your life. I will add unto you the fulfilment of promises, manifesting and materialising My Word in tangible ways for all to see. But you must always see that these outward blessings are just a shadow compared to the abundance of My life that can be known within your heart. This is the abundance that truly overwhelms the senses and blesses you because it is not external to you- it is Me in you. And I am with you wherever you go by My Spirit.

Come, dive in. Dive into the abundant life found only in Me and My Word, and let My life overflow within your heart.

SEE ALSO:

John 7:38 (NLT)
Anyone who believes in me may come and drink! For the Scriptures declare, 'Rivers of living water will flow from his heart.'

Proverbs 4:23 (AMP)
Watch over your heart with all diligence,
For from it flow the springs of life.

Deuteronomy 33:26 (AMP)
There is none like the God of Jeshurun (Israel), Who rides the heavens to your help, And through the skies in His majestic glory.

Psalm 148:13 (AMP)
Let them praise the name of the Lord, For His name alone is exalted and supreme; His glory and majesty are above earth and heaven.

Ephesians 3:20 (AMP)
Now to Him who is able to [carry out His purpose and] do superabundantly more than all that we dare ask or think [infinitely beyond our greatest prayers, hopes, or dreams], according to His power that is at work within us,

DAY 22:

I WANT TO ROMANCE YOU

> "My beloved spoke, and said to me:
> 'Rise up, my love, my fair one,
> And come away.'"
> Song of Solomon 2:10

Do you know the beauty of romance I have waiting for you every moment of every day? Romance is more than the giving of flowers or the writing of poems. That is how the world sees romance. True romance is the expression of love for another, however that so manifests. It is the giving of one's self. The more one gives them self to another, the more romance and intimacy is kindled. But do you know that romance is not just for the lovers, the husbands and wives, of this earth? This is just a precursor to the romance I long to share with you.

Do you know that I long to romance you? I long to delight your heart and express My passion for you. Why? Because you are My greatest love, the apple of My eye, the centre of all My affections, and I desire to see you satisfied by Me alone.

Look for how I romance you in the different pockets of your day. Look for the love notes I leave you through My creation, through your brothers and sisters, through those I speak through, and through My Word.

But do you know what the greatest expression of My love is for you? Do you know what the most romantic moment is in all of history, in all of creation? It was the moment I laid down My life for you, the one I love. This is true romance. My death and resurrection was the beginning of the most beautiful romance, the most epic love story, that the world has ever known.

I want to write on your heart My love story for you. Look to Me and let Me begin to romance you in ways you have never dreamed of. Come away with Me now.

SEE ALSO:

Song of Solomon 7:10
I am my beloved's,
And his desire is toward me.

1 John 4:9-10
In this the love of God was manifested toward us, that God has sent His only begotten Son into the world, that we might live through Him. In this is love, not that we loved God, but that He loved us and sent His Son to be the propitiation for our sins.

Hosea 2:14 (NLT)
But then I will win her back once again. I will lead her into the desert and speak tenderly to her there

1 John 3:16a
By this we know what love is: Jesus laid down His life for us...

Isaiah 62:5
*...And as the bridegroom rejoices over the bride,
So shall your God rejoice over you.*

DAY 23:
MY BEAUTIFUL SONG

"The Lord your God in your midst,
The Mighty One, will save;
He will rejoice over you with gladness,
He will quiet you with His love,
He will rejoice over you with singing."
Zephaniah 3:17

Do you know that your life is a song to Me? Your life is a beautiful song that I have composed in perfect harmony with Me. The song has already been written on your heart but can you read the music, can you hear the melody? Only when you look to Me can you sing along with Me for the song I have written for you, the song of your life, I am singing to you now. As you look to Me, you will hear Me singing this song, the beautiful song of your life. Oh, how sweet it is to My ears- when you are singing the song I have composed just for you!

I want every facet of your life to be in tune with the song I am singing over your now! May there be no clanging cymbals. The song I sing over you is the song of My love. Only when you are walking in love for Me are you singing to Me the song that I wrote for you. The beautiful song of your life is My love for you.

Worship is not just outward singing and praise, true worship is responding to My love for you. True worship is loving Me with all that you are as a response to My love for you. This is the greatest song I have ever written- a life laid down for Me in love. Can you sing Me the song I wrote for your life? Will you love Me with all that you are? For this is what I am singing over you now.

SEE ALSO:

1 Corinthians 13:1
Though I speak with the tongues of men and of angels, but have not love, I have become sounding brass or a clanging cymbal.

Ephesians 5:19 (AMP)
Speak to one another in psalms and hymns and spiritual songs, [offering praise by] singing and making melody with your heart to the Lord;

DAY 24:

MY GARDEN

"For the LORD will comfort Zion,
He will comfort all her waste places;
He will make her wilderness like Eden,
And her desert like the garden of the LORD;
Joy and gladness will be found in it,
Thanksgiving and the voice of melody."
Isaiah 51:3

You can liken the glory that is within Me to that of the most exquisite paradise, a garden full of the most beautiful flowers perfuming sweet fragrances in the air. Here in My garden you can find rest for your soul.

Where can you find this garden of My glory? It is within you. As this garden of My Presence grows in your heart, My joy and gladness will flow out of you. Thanksgiving and songs of praise will fill your lips.

But just as Adam in the Garden of Eden, I have given you responsibility to tend to My garden. I want you to nurture it so that My Presence in you may grow and blossom forth through you. My Spirit wants to beautify the inner chambers of your heart with the perfumed fragrances of heaven. As you keep your attention on Me by My Spirit, so My garden within you will grow, and My glory will be seen upon you. My fragrance will be diffused to those around you. This is the fragrance of heaven, the fragrance of My life to those who are perishing.

Like a flower in My garden, I want you to diffuse My fragrance and life wherever you go. Yet, unlike earthly flowers, you do not need ever to wilt or fade. You are not marked by seasons but by My Father's Word and purpose for you which are eternal. As long as you look to Me, you are in full bloom. So bloom radiantly in all My splendour and fill the earth with the fragrance of who I am!

SEE ALSO:

2 Corinthians 2: 14-15
Now thanks be to God who always leads us in triumph in Christ, and through us diffuses the fragrance of His knowledge in every place. For we are to God the fragrance of Christ among those who are being saved and among those who are perishing.

Song of Solngs 1:12 (TPT)
As the King surrounded me,
The sweet fragrance of my praise perfume
Awakened the night.

Luke 12:27
Consider the lilies, how they grow: they neither toil nor spin; and yet I say to you, even Solomon in all his glory was not arrayed like one of these.

Isaiah 40:8
The grass withers, the flower fades, But the word of our God stands forever

Song of Songs 7:12-13 (TPT)
*Let us arise and run to the vineyards of your people
And see if the budding vines of love
Are now in full bloom…
The love apples are in bloom,
Sending forth their fragrance of spring…*

DAY 25:

INNER BEAUTY

"...And when we see Him,
There is no beauty that we should desire Him."
Isaiah 53:2

The fullness of My beauty is not found in My appearance. It is found in My nature. It is found in My heart. It is found in what I have done for you and My love for you. That is where you see My ultimate beauty- it is hidden deep within Me, within who I AM.

I came to earth as a man with no outstanding beauty to the natural eye. I was considered by the world's standard ordinary in My physical appearance. But what drew the crowds to Me was the beauty within Me which radiated outwardly into My countenance. The glory of My Father, by the power of the Holy Spirit within Me, is what drew them. And this is what will draw you unto Me, the beauty and glory within My heart.

Now that I am seated in heaven, if I were to walk the earth in My glorified body, all would be drawn to Me, even just for My appearance. But right now, you do not see My beauty with your natural eyes, only by My

Spirit. False beauty can be seen with your eyes but cannot transcend any deeper. True beauty is known in your heart and changes you. It touches your inner being. True beauty is My beauty meeting with your heart.

When you focus more on the inward beauty of My nature the more My inner beauty will flourish through you. Your inner beauty coming forth is merely a reflection of the beauty you see in Me. For what you fix your eyes on, you reflect. You cannot reflect the beauty of My heart when you are fixated on what is outside of Me.

Always watch your heart when you are attempting to beautify the outward vessel or glory in your outer life. Do not be as the fallen angel Lucifer who gloried in his own beauty and splendour and then fell from heaven. Instead, focus on My inner beauty and watch it transcend into the depths of your being and then outwardly around you.

I came to the earth with no outward beauty yet crowds were drawn to Me. Are you trying to gain value and glory for your outward beauty or talent? When you try to adorn yourself with natural beauty or riches for your own glory, I cannot adorn you with Mine.

SEE ALSO:

Ezekiel 28:17 (AMP)
Your heart was proud and arrogant because of your beauty; You destroyed your wisdom for the sake of your splendor. I cast you to the ground; I lay you before kings, That they might look at you

Psalm 34:5
They looked to Him and were radiant, And their faces were not ashamed.

1 Peter 3:3-4
Do not let your adornment be merely outward—arranging the hair, wearing gold, or putting on fine apparel— rather let it be the hidden person of the heart, with the incorruptible beauty of a gentle and quiet spirit, which is very precious in the sight of God.

Psalm 90:17a
And let the beauty of the Lord our God be upon us...

DAY 26:

THE GREATEST SEPARATION

"He has delivered us from the power of darkness and conveyed us into the kingdom of the Son of His love, in whom we have redemption through His blood, the forgiveness of sins."
Colossians 1:13-14

When I died on the cross and rose again do you realise what separation took place? Do you realise the gulf that was formed? Oh, how deep! Oh, how wide! There is such a mighty gulf which now separates you from all evil, all sickness, all darkness, all fear, all discouragement and every vile thing. It is not on the perimeter or border of you. No- for when you were grafted into My body, all such things were separated far far far from you. No longer can you co-exist with them for I do not co-exist with sickness, I do not co-exist with sin, I do not co-exist with fear; I annihilate them! How far away are they from Me? As far as east is from the west!

Do you see My death and resurrection not only removed you from sin but from all evil power, sickness and torment? My blood separates you from all such things. Can you see the gulf now which separates you from these things? They are now wiped away so you have no need to live with them. Stay in the light of My Presence, focused on Me and see how far you are separated from all darkness. When you live abiding in the light and love of My glorious Presence, you will enjoy the freedom I enjoy. You will delight in the liberty and victory I possess.

SEE ALSO:

Romans 8:1-2
There is therefore now no condemnation to those who are in Christ Jesus, who do not walk according to the flesh, but according to the Spirit. For the law of the Spirit of life in Christ Jesus has made me free from the law of sin and death.

Psalm 103:11-12
For as the heavens are high above the earth,
So great is His mercy toward those who fear Him;
As far as the east is from the west,
So far has He removed our transgressions from us.

Colossians 2: 14-15 (NLT)
He cancelled the record of the charges against us and took it away by nailing it to the cross. In this way, he disarmed the spiritual rulers and authorities. He shamed them publicly by his victory over them on the cross

DAY 27:

TO KNOW ME IS TO FEAR ME

*"The secret of the L*ORD *is with those who fear Him,
And He will show them His covenant."*
Psalm 25:14

The light of My Presence comforts and brings peace yet it is in total opposition with darkness. I do not dwell with darkness; I expel it. You must choose whom you will serve: light or darkness: Myself, in the light of My Presence, or the darkness of sin.

The more you come to know Me, the more you will see that I am King and Lord, but I am also the righteous Judge. I am to be feared with holy trembling. Such terror should not draw you away from Me but rather draw you to Me, for those who continually turn away from the darkness of sin unto Me, will not experience My judgement. In Me, is righteousness, peace and freedom. In Me, you will experience My everlasting love and great mercy. You will experience the wonders of heaven's abundance. Apart from Me is where you do not want to be. Apart from Me is darkness and judgment and where there is no repentance- eternal torment.

Embrace My invitation to you to come into the light of My Presence and experience the freedom I give you from all darkness and sin. Do not reject My daily invitation to abide in Me. Allow My Spirit to empower you to follow Me in daily righteousness.

If you continue to practice sin in wilful disobedience, you will find when your days on this earth are over that the door to heaven you thought was open for you is shut. Only My judgement will await you. Do not let this be you! Continually accept My beckoning and wooing unto you to come to Me, to turn away from the world and sin and turn to Me. This is My desire for all. Come into My glorious light! Come and share in the delights of heaven found in My heart and never leave!

SEE ALSO:

Psalm 33:8
Let all the earth fear the Lord; Let all the inhabitants of the world stand in awe of Him

Matthew 7: 21-23

"Not everyone who says to Me, 'Lord, Lord,' shall enter the kingdom of heaven, but he who does the will of My Father in heaven. Many will say to Me in that day, 'Lord, Lord, have we not prophesied in Your name, cast out demons in Your name, and done many wonders in Your name?' And then I will declare to them, 'I never knew you; depart from Me, you who practice lawlessness!'

1 John 1:5-6

This is the message which we have heard from Him and declare to you, that God is light and in Him is no darkness at all. If we say that we have fellowship with Him, and walk in darkness, we lie and do not practice the truth.

Hebrews 10:30

*For we know Him who said, "Vengeance is Mine, I will repay," says the Lord. And again, "The L*ORD *will judge His people."*

DAY 28:

I AM THE WAY!

"Jesus said to him, 'I am the way, the truth, and the life. No one comes to the Father except through Me.'"
John 14:6

I am the way, the one and only way. I am the only way to the Father, the only way to peace. The only way to true satisfaction. The only way to victory.

So many see Me as the WAY to heaven, but they stop there. They look for other ways to find fulfilment and success in this life, yet they are left wanting. They fail to see that all true victory comes through Me. I am the only WAY to true satisfaction and contentment in your life. I am not an optional path. I AM THE WAY. Unless you walk with Me, following ME who is the WAY by My Spirit, you will fail. For without Me, you can do nothing. Your efforts will all be in vain.

When you are unfulfilled and restless, do not try to make changes in your life that I have not authored. Look to Me for the newness and refreshment you desire. I am the NEW, and I will work forth in you the newness that you long for. It will come through Me.

Keep your faith and hope in Me for your breakthrough.

Why are you striving and toiling, trying to bring down mountains and walls that I already demolished at Calvary? I have already broken through for you for I AM YOUR BREAKTHROUGH. I have already conquered all for I AM YOUR CONQUERER. Can't you see? There are no walls which stand between you and the Father's will except your lack of faith. Surrender to Me, and you will see that wall that you have erected through your doubts and fears has no power. Let me replace each brick with a new foundation, with Me as your cornerstone.

But do not seek Me for just your breakthrough. True breakthrough comes when you are not seeking a solution but when you are immersing yourself in the Solution, My very Presence. Simply delight in My Presence and the way you must go in this life will be made simple. Enjoy Me and as you walk daily in love with Me all else will be given to you. The answer to all who are looking for "the way" is simply enjoying the life of My Presence in you. I am the Way, the Truth and the Life; I am LIFE itself. Meet with Me, enjoy Me and you will come to know by My Spirit all you need in this life and the life to come.

SEE ALSO:

Romans 8:37
Yet in all these things we are more than conquerors through Him who loved us.

1 Corinthians 3:10-14
According to the grace of God which was given to me, as a wise master builder I have laid the foundation, and another builds on it. But let each one take heed how he builds on it. For no other foundation can anyone lay than that which is laid, which is Jesus Christ. Now if anyone builds on this foundation with gold, silver, precious stones, wood, hay, straw, each one's work will become clear; for the Day will declare it, because it will be revealed by fire; and the fire will test each one's work, of what sort it is. If anyone's work which he has built on it endures, he will receive a reward.

Psalm 37:3-4
Trust in the LORD, and do good;
Dwell in the land, and feed on His faithfulness.
Delight yourself also in the LORD,
And He shall give you the desires of your heart.

Psalm 23: 1 (NLT)
The LORD is my shepherd; I have all that I need

YOUR INVITATION TO KNOW JESUS CHRIST

Jesus wants to share His abundant life with you every moment of every day. He is longing for you to come to Him so you may be filled with the delight of His life-giving Presence and the glorious power of His Spirit, having deep and satisfying communion with God the Father, Son and Holy Spirit forevermore. But, since the fall of Adam in the Garden of Eden, one thing separates you from having this fellowship with God- sin. The Word of God declares that we all have sinned and fallen short of experiencing the glory of God (Romans 3:23) and that because of our sin, we are all deserving of hell (Romans 6:23). The only thing that can cleanse us from our sin and give us a new righteous life is the death and resurrection of Jesus.

"For the wages of sin is death, but the gift of God is eternal life in Christ Jesus our Lord." (Romans 6:23)

The Son of God, Jesus, whom you have read in this devotional was perfect and without sin. He came down from heaven as a man and humbled Himself to die for your sins. Three days later He was raised from the dead, overcoming all the power of sin and darkness. Now, whoever believes in Jesus and turns from their sin unto Him, is forgiven and can enjoy an intimate relationship with God the Father, Son and Holy Spirit, now and for all eternity (John 3:16).

Through the sacrifice He made, Jesus wants to replace your old sinful life with the newness and splendour of His. This is what it truly means to be born again. You become a new creation born of God and enter God's family. Your old life passes away and all things become new. The wondrous life and beauty of Jesus can now begin to flow through you!

It doesn't matter if you have been to church your whole life or never before, the only way to come to know God and experience His amazing life, is to turn away from your sin and give your life now to Jesus.

If you want to accept God's invitation and receive this new life through what Jesus Christ has done for you, simply pray the following prayer with all your heart:

Dear Jesus,

I believe You are the Son of God and I want to know You. Thank You for coming to earth to die and rise again for me.

I turn away from all my sin and my old life and surrender my life completely to You now. Come into my heart and cleanse me with Your precious blood. I receive Your forgiveness.

Jesus, You are now my Saviour and Lord. I belong to You; my heart is Yours forever. God Almighty, You are my Heavenly Father and I am Your child. I am now born again!

Fill me with Your Holy Spirit. I give You permission to have Your way in every area of my life. Help me to live every day to please You alone by the power You provide.

In Jesus name, I pray, Amen.

If you prayed this prayer with all your heart-congratulations! You have no idea the wonder and delight that await you as you come to know God through the life of Jesus!

The Word says that we must confess our faith in Jesus (Romans 10:9). If you prayed this prayer, I encourage you to tell someone (preferably someone who also has a relationship with Jesus) about this eternal decision. Find a Spirit-filled local church, get baptised with water and the Holy Spirit (Matthew 3:11; Acts 1:5), and read God's Word, the Bible, to learn more about who God is.

The fact that you have become born again into God's family does not mean that your life will suddenly be without problems or temptations. The difference is now, regardless of what circumstances you face, you can be confident that your Heavenly Father and Lord Jesus are with you, and surround you with Their love and protection. God also sent you the greatest gift to earth, the Holy Spirit, to be your personal Helper. He is ever present to comfort, help and lead you to victoriously overcome all temptation and evil which oppose you. As you depend on the Holy Spirit moment by moment and allow the life of Jesus to flow through you, you will experience a life of His righteousness, joy and peace.

Come now and embark on the most amazing journey of all- coming to experience for yourself the life and beauty of Jesus Christ!

One thing I have asked of the LORD, and that I will seek:
That I may dwell in the house of the LORD
[in His presence] all the days of my life,
To gaze upon the beauty
[the delightful loveliness and majestic grandeur]
of the LORD
And to meditate in His temple.

Psalm 27:4 (AMP)

OTHER BOOKS BY THIS AUTHOR

Heart of the Father

Available for free download at iTunes store

Heart of the Father 2

For more information visit:
www.facebook.com/heartofthefatherbook

www.ingramcontent.com/pod-product-compliance
Lightning Source LLC
Chambersburg PA
CBHW070548300426
44113CB00011B/1821